New Jersey Fish Species

Game Fish & Panfish

Billy Grinslott & Kinsey Marie Books

ISBN - 9781968228668

Banded Sunfish got their name because they have darker lines that run vertically on their sides. They also have a rounded tail with spots on their body, tail and fins. Banded sunfish are typically only about 2 inches long, making them one of the smallest sunfish. Their small size makes them vulnerable to larger fish, so they thrive in protected areas. Banded sunfish prefer slow-moving, vegetated waters like swamps, ponds, and backwaters of creeks.

The Green Sunfish is blue green in color. It has yellow flecks on both its scales and some parts of its sides. The Green Sunfish also has broken blue stripes which is why some people confuse it with the Bluegill. Green Sunfish are very adaptable. They can live in any body of water that has vegetation or weeds. Green sunfish are opportunistic feeders, consuming insects, small fish, and other invertebrates.

The Warmouth is a member of the Rock Bass, Green Sunfish and Bluegill family. They can survive in low oxygen environments while other fish cannot. Warmouth can thrive in muddy water, when other fish can't. Warmouth are often confused with rock bass. The difference between the two is in the anal fin: warmouth have three spines on the anal fin ray and rock bass have six spines.

The Blue spotted sunfish is a small freshwater fish known for its vibrant blue spots and tolerance for acidic low oxygen waters. They are native to the southeastern and eastern United States, inhabiting ponds, rivers, and backwaters with dense vegetation. They are one of the smallest fish in their family, typically reaching a maximum length of about 3.7 inches. Both males and females have light blue or white spots, but males tend to have more intense and vibrant spotting. They have a relatively short lifespan, typically living around 5 years.

The bluegill also considered a sunfish is the most popular fish to fish for. They are called pan fish because they are about the size of a frying pan. Bluegills love to eat insects and bugs. They have good vision and rely on their keen eyesight to feed. Three types in this group are the Bluegill, Sunfish, and Pumpkinseed.

The Pumpkinseed is also known as pond perch, sun perch, and punky's sunfish. It can be found in numerous lakes, ponds, and rivers. It is their body shape resembling the seed of a pumpkin, that inspired their name. Pumpkinseed sunfish have speckles on their orangish colored sides and back, with a yellow to orange belly and chest. They are active during the day and rest at night near the bottom or in shelter areas.

The Redbreast sunfish has a red-yellow chest and belly with rusty brown spots on their body. The species is known for its distinctive grunting vocalizations, which are produced by grinding their teeth together. Redbreast sunfish can survive in oxygen-poor environments by using their gills to extract oxygen from air bubbles trapped in aquatic vegetation.

The Mud Sunfish is a secretive, small freshwater fish known for its stocky body, large mouth, and distinctive dark stripes. It prefers to live in slow-moving, tannin-stained waters like swamps, bogs, ponds, and backwaters with soft, silty bottoms and aquatic plants. Their color ranges from olive to brownish tan. They are usually small, rarely exceeding 6 to 8 inches in length.

The American shad is the largest species in the herring family. They are known for a delicate, rich flavor, often described as oily or like sardines. They can grow up to 30 inches and weigh up to 12 pounds. They have a metallic blue/green back, silver sides, a deeply forked tail, and a row of dark spots behind the gill flap. They prefer freshwater rivers for spawning and the Atlantic Ocean for feeding, often traveling hundreds of miles upstream. The largest American shad officially recorded in New Jersey weighed 11 pounds, 1 ounce.

Fallfish are the largest native minnow species in eastern North America, often reaching 15-18 inches in length and weighing over 2 pounds, inhabiting clear, rocky streams. They are known for building massive, pyramid-shaped nests from rocks, with males creating structures that can reach 6 feet in diameter and weigh up to 2 tons. They are silvery with dark-edged scales, a dark stripe along the back, and a large, blunt snout.

White perch grow seven to ten inches in length and rarely weigh more than one pound. They have a silvery body with faint lines on the sides. The white perch is an opportunistic feeder. Young feed primarily on zooplankton and adults feed on aquatic insect larvae, minnows and fish eggs. White Perch is a euryhaline species, inhabiting fresh, brackish and coastal waters. The largest white perch caught in New Jersey is a 3-pound, 1-ounce fish.

The two most famous perches are the common perch and the yellow perch. The yellow perch has a brilliant greenish yellow color with orange fins. The yellow perch is the biggest one and can grow to a size of 18 inches. It's also known as the jumbo perch. The other type of perch is the white perch. The largest yellow perch caught in New Jersey weighed 4 pounds, 3 ounces and measured 18 inches.

The Rock Bass is not actually a bass but a member of the sunfish family. They are commonly known as redeyes, due to their bright red to orangish iris, and are sometimes confused as smallmouth bass or warmouth. Rock bass prefer waters with rocky vegetated areas, that's how they got their name. The biggest Rock Bass ever caught on record weighs about three pounds and was a little over one foot long.

There are two main types of crappies. The white crappie and the black crappie. They are also members of the sunfish family. The difference between the white and black crappie is one has dark spots and the other has dark lines and is lighter in color. The white crappie has six dorsal fin spines, whereas the black crappie has eight dorsal fin spines. The white crappie can grow bigger and more of the bigger white crappie are caught in North America. The largest black crappie caught in New Jersey weighed 4 pounds, 8 ounces.

The sucker fish has the same mouth as a carp. They got their name because their mouth is like a suction cup. They normally are bottom feeders and suck their food from the bottom of the lake. Many people use sucker fish to fish for northern pike and other big game fish. Typically, 12–20 inches long, these hardy, bottom-dwelling fish inhabit diverse, often polluted, water bodies, where they eat invertebrates, algae, and eggs.

The black, brown and yellow bullhead are part of the catfish family. They usually only grow to about 10 inches long. They use their whiskers to help find food. The bullhead is the most common member of the catfish family. Bullheads live in the water containing low oxygen levels. They can survive on low oxygen areas, where other fish can't. Based on available records, the largest recorded brown bullhead in New Jersey is a 5.45-pound fish.

Flathead Catfish, their body is wide but flattened and very low in height. Both eyes are on the top of the flattened head, giving excellent vision to see upward. Flathead catfish live mainly in large bodies of water like big rivers and reservoirs. They prefer deep pools. The largest Flathead Catfish caught in the area was a 72.5-pound, 50-inch fish.

The Channel Catfish are the most fished catfish species with around 8 million anglers fishing for them per year. Channel catfish have taste buds all over their body, making them highly sensitive to the taste and smell of food. They also have barbels (whiskers) around their mouths, which are used for sensing and tasting food. They use sound waves to communicate with each other. They can also produce alarm substances to warn other catfish of danger. The largest Channel Catfish caught in New Jersey weighed 33 pounds, 3 ounces.

The stonecat is a slender, freshwater catfish known for its preference for living in fast moving streams and rivers. They are often found under rocks and boulders in riffles. Stonecats have a long, thin body with a rounded or slightly forked tail. Their color varies, typically ranging from tan to gray on the back and sides, with a lighter belly. Stonecats are primarily active at night, feeding on insects, fish eggs, and small fish. Stonecats typically reach 4 to 8 inches in length and weigh up to 1 pound.

There are several species of catfish. Blue catfish are known for their size, reaching over 100 pounds. Blue catfish, like other catfish, lack scales and have smooth skin. They have barbels (whiskers) around their mouths, which are used for sensing and tasting food. They are generally slate blue on the back and silvery/white on the underside. Blue Catfish are being reintroduced to New Jersey but haven't yet produced record sizes yet.

White catfish are interesting because they are smaller than other common catfish species like channel catfish, they have a wider head and lack the black spots of channel catfish. White catfish are the smallest of the large North American catfish species. The White catfish has white chin barbells, which distinguish it from other species. There are four pairs of barbels, whiskers around the mouth, two on the chin, one at the angle of the mouth, and one behind the nostril. The largest White Catfish caught in New Jersey weighed 14 pounds, 4 ounces.

The madtom is a small catfish that is native to the eastern United States. Madtoms are scaleless fishes with eight whisker-like barbels around their mouths used as sensors. The madtom feeds on the bottom at night, using its sensitive barbels, whiskers to touch and taste for food. Its diet consists mostly of aquatic insects. Madtoms are small catfishes that generally measure between 2 and 6 inches in length.

Sculpins are small, bottom-dwelling fish with a flattened body shape, large pectoral fins, and a unique camouflage pattern, often found in clear, fast-flowing waters with rocky substrates, and they are known for their ambush hunting tactics. Sculpins have very large mouths and can swallow items nearly as large as themselves. Many sculpins have venomous spines along their fins, with particularly dangerous spines on their gill covers, used for defense.

Bowfins have a specialized gas bladder that functions as a lung, allowing them to breathe air and survive in stagnant, low-oxygen water where other fish cannot. Bowfins are often described as prehistoric relics. This is because the species can be traced to fossils from the Cretaceous, Eocene and Jurassic period. The largest bowfin caught in New Jersey is a 12-pound, 10-ounce fish.

The Hybrid Striped Bass is a cross between a male White Bass and a female Striped Bass, known for its broken stripes, deep body, and excellent fighting ability. It's a favorite game fish in many freshwater reservoirs, prized for its aggressive nature, often caught with spoons, jigs, or live bait, especially in cooler months. They are sterile and do not reproduce naturally, so they are stocked in lakes and rivers by state hatcheries. They can grow to significant sizes, often reaching several pounds within three years. The largest hybrid striped bass caught in New Jersey is a 17-pound, 12-ounce fish.

Striped bass are often called Stripers. Striped bass live in both salt and fresh water. Striped bass have very sensitive eyes and will seek deep water when the sun is out. Striped bass have a preferred water temperature range of from 55° F to 68° F, and swim to find water of these temperatures. White Bass are related to Striped Bass and have lighter stripes on their sides. The largest striped bass caught in New Jersey is a 78-pound, 8-ounce fish.

Sturgeons have sharp spines on their back, so be careful when handling them. Instead of scales, sturgeon skin is covered in bony plates called scutes, which can be very sharp on young sturgeon. Sturgeons have been around since the dinosaur days. Sturgeons mostly live in large, freshwater lakes and rivers. Their average lifespan is 50 to 60 years. A massive 220-pound, 6-foot-long Atlantic sturgeon was captured and released in July 2024.

There are few different species of Gar, the Longnose gar, Short nose and Alligator gar. The Long Nose Gar got its name because of its long mouth that looks like an alligator's mouth. The alligator gar is one of the biggest freshwater fish growing up to 10 feet long. The world record for a catch was set at 327 pounds. Longnose gar typically measure 2 to 3 feet in length and weigh around 4 to 10 pounds.

The American eel is North America's only freshwater eel, known for its snake-like body, and ability to live in freshwater. They have a Snake-like body, dark on top (green/brown) with yellowish sides and a pale belly. They have a continuous fin that runs along the length of their whole back. They use their whole body to swim and can slither like a snake over the ground and obstacles. They are most active at night and hide during the day, under rocks or burying themselves into the sediment at the bottom. The largest American eel ever recorded in New Jersey was a 9-pound, 13-ounce fish.

Snakehead fish are known as walking fish, because they can move on land for days by wiggling with their fins and body. They can breathe air with lung-like organs, allowing them to survive out of water for days and even crawl to new water bodies using their fins. They can also burrow into the mud and hibernate during cold weather or dry spells. They thrive in various slow-moving, shallow, vegetated waters, like ponds, swamps, and streams, and can survive in low oxygen levels. The largest Snakehead fish caught in New Jersey was 13.55 pounds.

Male freshwater drum also known as sheepshead make a rumbling or grunting sound by contracting muscles along their air bladder walls. They have large, ivory-like ear bones that can be up to an inch in diameter, which Native Americans used as necklaces or bracelets and sometimes referred to as the lucky stones. Freshwater drum are primarily bottom feeders, spending much of their time near the bottom of lakes and rivers in search of food. The largest black drum fish caught in New Jersey is a 109-pound fish.

Carp have long been an important food fish to humans. Carp are bottom feeders for the most part and their mouth is made like a suction cup, so they can suck food off the bottom. Carp are good for a lake because they help clean the bottom of the lake. The largest carp recorded in New Jersey is a 76-pound, 11-ounce Grass Carp.

The rainbow trout gets its name because of its brilliant colors. Rainbow trout populations are good indicators of water pollution because they can only survive in clean waters. They like to live in rivers and streams. Rainbow trout rank among the top five most sought game fish in North America. The largest rainbow trout recorded in New Jersey weighed 13 pounds.

Tiger trout are known for their aggressive nature and awesome looking tiger-like stripes. Tiger trout are not naturally occurring in the wild, but rather a hybrid created by mixing a female brown trout with a male brook trout. They are stocked in lakes and rivers. Their striking appearance with tiger-like stripes and patterns, makes them easily recognizable. They are known to grow faster than their parent species. Tiger trout typically measure 10–16 inches and weigh 1–3 pounds.

The lake trout is one of the biggest of the trout family. The biggest lake trout caught was 72 pounds. Lake trout like to live in lakes that are deep. They like being in the cool water in the deep parts of a lake. They have been reported to live up to 70 years in some Canadian lakes. The largest lake trout ever recorded in New Jersey was a 32-pound, 11-ounce fish.

Brook trout are characterized by their olive-green bodies with pale, worm-like markings, red spots with bluish halos, and orange-red fins with white and black edges. They can grow up to 12 inches in length. Brook trout are cold-water fish that prefer clean, clear, and cold streams, lakes, and ponds. The largest Brook trout caught in New Jersey is a 7-pound, 3-ounce fish.

Brown trout can live up to 20 years. Brown trout have higher tolerance for warmer waters than either brook or rainbow trout. Brown trout can be found on almost every continent except Antarctica, and many can be found living in the ocean. The largest Brown trout caught in New Jersey is a 21-pound, 6-ounce fish.

Smallmouth bass have a smaller mouth than the largemouth bass. They also have different markings and are lighter in color. They don't live in most lakes because they prefer living in colder water. They are typically found in the northern states in America because the water is cooler. The current world record smallmouth is an 11-pound, 15-ounce fish. They can be found in lakes, reservoirs, and rivers. The largest smallmouth bass caught in New Jersey is a 7-pound, 2-ounce fish.

The largemouth bass is the most sought-after bass in North America. Largemouth bass live in just about every lake in North America. They have great hearing and can hear a crayfish crawling on the bottom of the lake. The largest largemouth bass caught in New Jersey is a 10-pound, 14-ounce fish.

The walleye got its name because of its white looking eyes. Their eyes collect light, even in low light conditions. This means they can see in the dark. Because they can see in the dark, they mostly feed at night. During the daytime their eyes are very sensitive, so they usually head for deeper water or shady places. Walleye like to live in cooler water and are normally found in the upper part of North America. The largest walleye officially recorded in New Jersey is a 13-pound, 9-ounce fish.

Pickerel kind of look like northern pike, but they are not. The Pike is larger in size than the Pickerel. The Pickerel has more spots than the Pike, but the Pike has spots on its fins and pickerel don't. Pickerel has a dark bar beneath their eyes and northern pike don't. Pickerel are also known as gunfish or slime darts. The largest Chain Pickerel caught in New Jersey is a 9-pound, 6-ounce fish.

The Redfin Pickerel is a small, solitary freshwater fish in the pike family, typically measuring 10–15 inches and living 8–10 years. They inhabit clear, slow-moving, heavily vegetated streams and swamps. They are ambush predators feeding on small fish, crustaceans, and insects. They are olive to yellowish green with distinct, bright red-orange fins and a dark, backwards-slanting bar beneath the eye.

The Northern Pike is one of the most sought-after fish for anglers. It got its name because it likes to live in cooler water mainly in the northern states of North America. The northern pike is a very aggressive predator. They don't like to live in groups with other fish, they are very territorial and like to live alone. Their behavior is closely affected by weather conditions. The largest Northern Pike caught in New Jersey is a 30-pound, 8.5-ounce fish.

The muskellunge called the Musky or Muskie for short is one of the biggest game fish in freshwater lakes. The largest on record was 69 pounds, 15 ounces. The Muskie likes to live in cooler water and can be found in most lakes in the upper part of north America. Anglers look at Muskellunges as trophy fish. They are hard to catch. There's a saying that it takes a thousand casts to catch one. The largest muskellunge caught in New Jersey is a 42 pound, 13-ounce fish.

Another breed of the Muskie is the tiger musky. The tiger muskie is a cross between the northern pike and muskie. They grow larger and faster than normal muskies and northern pikes. The tiger muskie got its name because it has tiger like stripes. Tiger Muskies are very rare and hard to catch. The world record tiger muskie is a massive fish weighing 51 pounds, 3 ounces. The largest tiger muskie caught in New Jersey is a 29-pound fish.

Author Page

Billy Grinslott & Kinsey Marie Books

ISBN – 9781968228668

Thanks